THE A-TEAM PRESENTS...
Top Secret Mission #3

Jack Gets Too Silly

Authored by
Courtney Butorac

Illustrations by
Emily Zieroth

Produced by PBL Consulting
936 NW 57th St
Seattle, WA 98107
www.sociallearning.org

Please contact
PBL Consulting at
info@pblconsulting.org
for more information.
Copyright 2016.
All rights reserved.

When forms and sample documents are included, their use is authorized only by educators, local school sites, and/or noncommercial or nonprofit entities who have purchased the book or have received a book by attending a workshop. Except for that usage, no part of this book may be reproduced or utilized in any form or by any means, electronic or mechanical, including photocopying, recording or by any information storage or retrieval system, without permission in writing by the publisher.

Sometimes I make silly faces or jokes in class. Sometimes, I duck walk around the classroom or act like robot when the teacher calls on me. Lots of people laugh when I do these things. But, my teacher told me the other day that it wasn't funny anymore. I disagreed because the other kids in class were laughing! If it wasn't funny, they wouldn't laugh.

On Tuesday, in art class, I was sitting across from my friend Max. I felt like being silly, so I made my face look like a zombie.

Max made a weird face back and I started laughing.

The teacher looked at me and told me to be quiet. I made a zipping sound with my mouth to show her I had zipped my lip and threw away the key. The kids in the class giggled.

On Friday, while we were reading, it was really quiet. Too quiet. So, I decided to make my friend Alex laugh. I got his attention and made a really silly face at him. He smiled, but then went right back to reading. I tried again. "Stop, Jack," he whispered, "I'm reading." I really wanted to make him laugh, so I told him a joke, "how do you make a tissue dance? Put a little boogey in it!"
He laughed out loud. It worked!

That afternoon I met with my friendship group - the A-Team. We get together to learn about social skills and to help each other when we have challenges with friends or in class.

"Welcome everyone! Does anyone have anything to talk about?" Ms. Corina asked us.

"Yeah," Alex said, "I got in trouble because of Jack today."

"Hey, you laughed at my joke! I didn't get you in trouble," I defended myself.

"But you are always being silly in class," Lily added.

"Well, people laugh when I am silly. What's wrong with that?" I asked.

"Sometimes I can't concentrate when you are being so silly," Max said.

"Oh," I said. "But I like telling jokes!"

"Well," said Ms. Corina, "you ARE really funny and you DO like to make people laugh, which we love. But, how do you think it makes the teacher feel when you make a joke in class when she is trying to teach?"

I thought about Ms. Miller and the looks she had been giving me this week.

"I guess she feels upset," I said.

Ms. Corina agreed, "it's important that we think about how our actions affect other people. When you act too silly at the wrong times, it can make other people feel uncomfortable or annoyed.

"When you are TOO silly, it can be disruptive to the class, which makes learning hard for everyone, even your friends."

I thought some more about what happened with Alex earlier. Alex usually thinks I'm funny, but my silliness got him in trouble. He was trying to read, and I was distracting him from his work. And, I wasn't doing my work either. I looked at Alex and apologized.

Alex said, "I do think you are really funny, but was trying to read!"

"But, Ms. Corina, I just like having others pay attention to me in class. When I am funny, people usually laugh. I like that attention."

When it's okay to be silly:

- During recess or lunch
- At home, during a play date with a friend
- On the weekends
- During free time in class

Other strategies:

- Talk to your teacher when you might be able to be silly.
- Ask your teacher to give you a signal to remind you to focus
- Use a visual check in to see how silly others are being and whether the teacher is smiling about it.

"Now, let's talk about how to get positive attention from your friends and teachers."

How to get positive attention from your friends and teachers:

"Ok, Jack, you now have your top secret mission for next week. This weekend, talk more with your parents about the places where it's okay to be silly and practice getting attention in other ways. On Monday, it will be time for you to complete your Top Secret Mission at school.

Do you accept your mission?" Ms Corina asked.

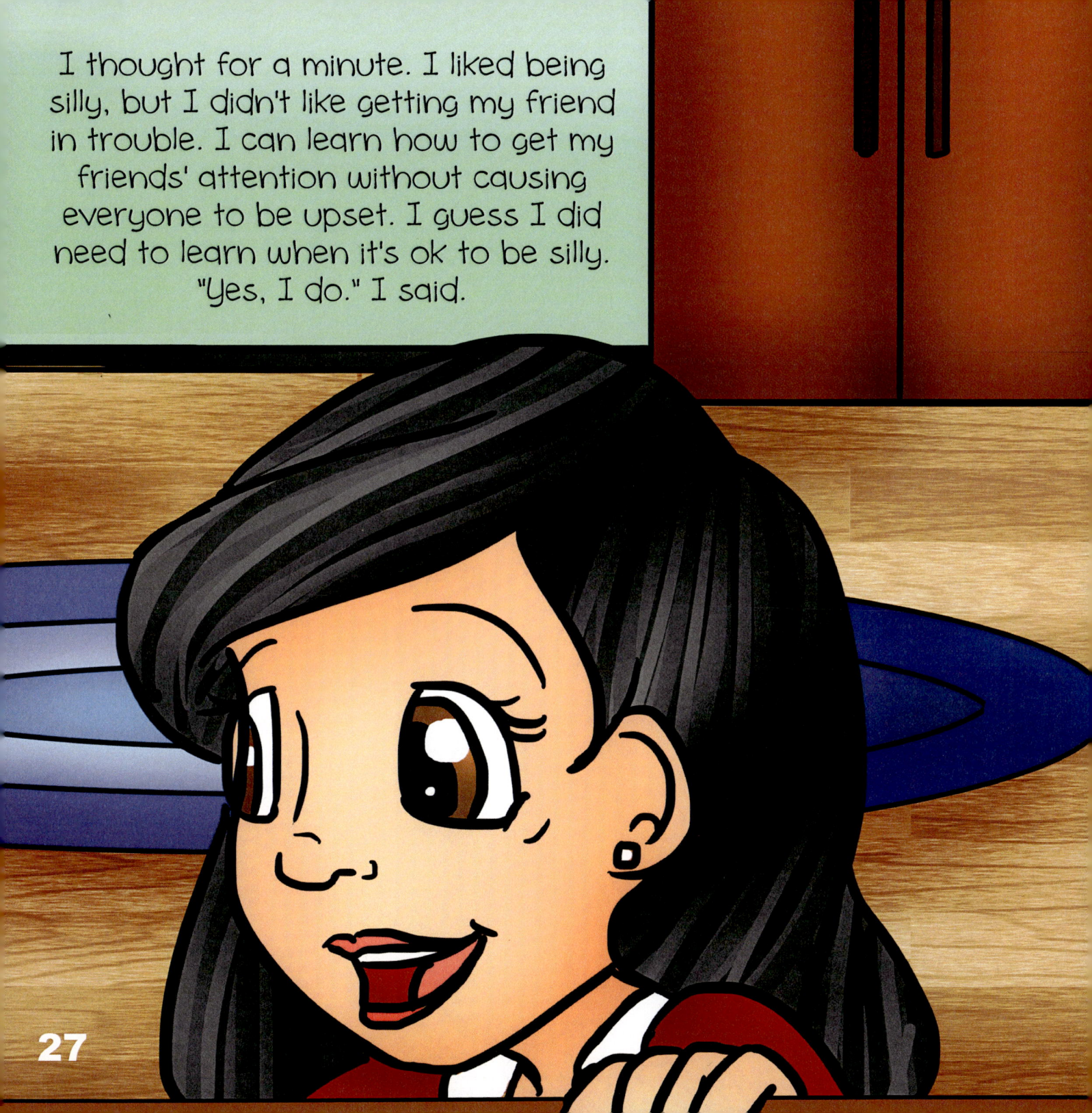

I'm so glad I was able to figure out how to get positive attention from my friends and when it's okay to be silly.

I wonder what my next top secret mission will be....

ABOUT THE AUTHOR

Courtney Butorac

Courtney Butorac has been supporting kids and adults with autism and also their families for 25 years as an elementary school special education teacher, preschool teacher, camp counselor and behavioral therapist. She has pioneered new ways to support social learning within her school district and is an enthusiastic member of a behavior and autism intervention team that engages district-wide to help teachers develop the knowledge and tools to support students with autism in their classrooms. Courtney has designed and facilitated powerful professional learning for educators that focuses on how to teach social skills to students with a broad range of disabilities and how to support behavioral needs in the classroom. Additionally, Courtney has guest lectured multiple times at the University of Washington's early childhood special education program.

Years ago, she and a group of her students with autism formed the A-Team friendship group to tackle the common social challenges facing her kids. These students helped inspire the "The A-Team Presents..." characters and book series.

Courtney has both a Master's Degree in early childhood special education and her Board Certification in Behavior Analysis (BCBA).

Courtney lives in Seattle with her husband, who is a fellow educator, and two young and energetic sons.

Explore more books about various social challenges in "The A-Team" book series!

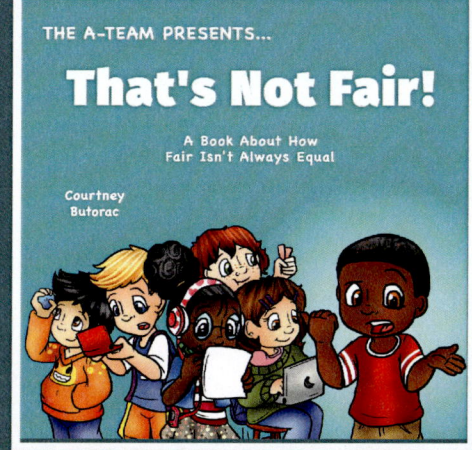
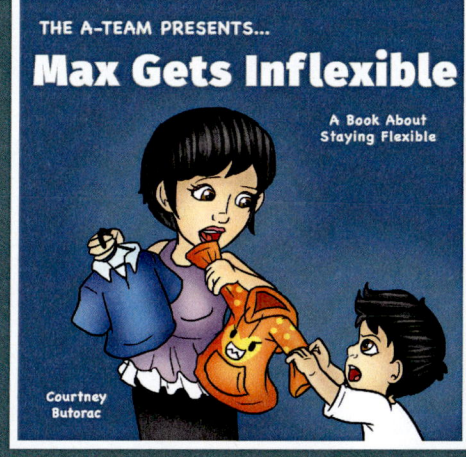

Find useful, free resources on the web at sociallearning.org

Made in the USA
San Bernardino, CA
07 September 2017